PEYTON MANNING

By Ryan Nagelhout

Gareth Stevens
Publishing

RIGHT ON!

Please visit our website www.garethstevens.com. For a free color catalog of all our high-quality books, call toll free 1-800-542-2595 or fax 1-877-542-2596.

Library of Congress Cataloging-in-Publication Data

Nagelhout, Ryan.
Peyton Manning / by Ryan Nagelhout.
  p. cm. — (Today's great quarterbacks)
Includes index.
ISBN 978-1-4824-0480-7 (pbk.)
ISBN 978-1-4824-0481-4 (6-pack)
ISBN 978-1-4824-0478-4 (library binding)
1. Manning, Peyton — Juvenile literature. 2. Football players — United States — Biography — Juvenile literature. 3. Quarterbacks (Football) — United States — Biography — Juvenile literature. I. Nagelhout, Ryan. II. Title.
GV939.M289 N34 2014
796.332092—dc23

First Edition

Published in 2014 by
Gareth Stevens Publishing
111 East 14th Street, Suite 349
New York, NY 10003

Copyright © 2014 Gareth Stevens Publishing

Designer: Nicholas Domiano
Editor: Ryan Nagelhout

Photo credits: Cover, p. 1 John Grieshop/Getty Images Sport/Getty Images; pp. 5, 25 Kevin Mazur/WireImage/Getty Images; pp. 7, 11 Bill Frakes/Sports Illustrated/Getty Images; p. 9 Sporting News/Getty Images; p. 13 Scott Halleran/Hulton Archive/Getty Images; p. 15 Ezra Shaw/Hulton Archive/Getty Images; p. 17 Jonathan Daniel/Getty Images Sport/Getty Images; p. 19 Jed Jacobsohn/Getty Images Sport/Getty Images; p. 21 Jim Rogash/Getty Images Sport/Getty Images; p. 23 Michael Zagaris/Getty Images Sport/Getty Images; p. 27 Justin Edmonds/Getty Images Sport/Getty Images; p. 29 Mark Mainz/Getty Images Entertainment/Getty Images.

Printed in the United States of America

CPSIA compliance information: Batch #CW14GS: For further information contact Gareth Stevens, New York, New York at 1-800-542-2595.

CONTENTS

Meet Peyton

Peyton Manning is a **National Football League** (NFL) superstar! He's a great quarterback.

Peyton Williams Manning was born on March 24, 1976, in New Orleans, Louisiana. His parents are Olivia and Archie Manning. Peyton grew up in New Orleans.

Football Family

The Manning family loves football! Peyton's dad, Archie, played quarterback for the New Orleans Saints. His younger brother, Eli, plays for the New York Giants.

Peyton Manning

Archie Manning

Eli Manning

Peyton played quarterback at Isadore Newman School. Many **colleges** wanted him to play for them. He picked the University of Tennessee.

Volunteers Great

Peyton had a great college **career** with the Tennessee Volunteers. He started at quarterback all 4 years. Peyton's number 16 was **retired** by Tennessee.

Peyton was considered a top **prospect** by NFL scouts. He was picked first overall by the Indianapolis Colts in the 1998 NFL Draft.

Colts Quarterback

Peyton started his Colts career in 1998. He started at quarterback right away! Peyton made the playoffs with the Colts in 2002.

Peyton was named NFL Most Valuable Player (MVP) in 2003 and 2004. He won the award four times with the Colts.

19

Super Colts

In 2007, Peyton led the Colts against the Chicago Bears in Super Bowl 41. The Colts won, 29-17. Peyton was named the game's MVP!

21

Second Super Bowl

Peyton had a great season in 2009. He led the Colts to another Super Bowl! On February 7, 2010, the Colts lost to the New Orleans Saints, 31-17, in Super Bowl 44.

23

Peyton missed all of the 2011 season because of a neck injury. In 2012, he won the Comeback Player of the Year Award.

New Team

In 2012, the Colts drafted Stanford quarterback Andrew Luck. Peyton was **released** by the Colts. He had to find a new team!

What's Next?

In March 2012, Peyton signed with the Denver Broncos. He's playing with a new team now. What will he do next?

Timeline

1976   Peyton is born on March 24.

1995   Peyton starts at quarterback for the University of Tennessee.

1998   The Indianapolis Colts draft Peyton first overall.

He starts for the Colts in his first season.

2003   Peyton wins his first of 4 NFL MVP awards.

2007   Peyton wins Super Bowl 41 with the Colts.

2010   Peyton leads Colts to Super Bowl 44.

2012   Peyton is released by the Colts. He signs with the Denver Broncos.

Peyton wins Comeback Player of the Year Award.

Books

Sandler, Michael. *Peyton Manning*. New York, NY: Bearport Publishing, 2012.

Tieck, Sarah. *Peyton Manning*. Edina, MN: ABDO Publishing Co., 2011.

Websites

PeyBack Foundation

peytonmanning.com
Find out more about Peyton's charity at his personal website.

Peyton Manning's NFL Player Page

nfl.com/player/peytonmanning/2501863/profile
Take a look at Peyton's stats and biography on his NFL player page.

Glossary

career: the job someone chooses to do for a long time

college: a school after high school

National Football League: the top football league in the United States

prospect: a player likely to play in the NFL

released: fired from a job

retired: no longer in use

Index